UP THE NILE

A PHOTOGRAPHIC EXCURSION: EGYPT 1839–1898

Deborah Bull and Donald Lorimer

Foreword by Anne Horton

Photographs, Sotheby Parke Bernet

Clarkson N. Potter, Inc./Publishers   New York
Distributed by Crown Publishers, Inc.

Acknowledgments

It would have been impossible to do this book without the generous help of many individuals, libraries, and museums. We warmly thank all of those who gave us their time and made their photographs available to us for research and for reproduction in this book.

For their support from the beginning, and for their continuous help, we especially thank Anne Horton and Peter Coffeen. We are deeply grateful to Diane Guzman, Librarian of the Wilbour Library of Egyptology, and the entire staff of the Department of Egyptian and Classical Art at the Brooklyn Museum. From the beginning of our research, they made their original photographs and resources available to us, as well as giving us direction and advice.

We thank, with great pleasure, Gérard Lévy in Paris for his graciousness and generosity with his time, for sharing some of his photographs with us, and for his invaluable help and leads to other sources. We thank also François Braunschweig at Texbraun and François Lepage, assistant to Mr. Lévy. For help in our research, special thanks to Dr. Carney Gavin, Curator, and the staff of the Semitic Museum at Harvard. They are currently assembling a comprehensive photo-archive of the nineteenth-century Near East. We also acknowledge the contribution of Adam Weinberg's research on Sébah.

We are indebted to Sally Santosuosso at the Princeton University Library; May Ellen MacNamara at the Photographic Collection, Humanities Research Center at the University of Texas; Valerie Lloyd at the Royal Photographic Society; and Ms. Vogel at the James B. Ford Library at the Explorers Club for their courtesy and help.

There are others to whom special thanks are due: Scott Hyde, who provided us with beautiful copy prints of many of the original photographs; Betsy Bryan for her assistance with the Egyptology; Mary Flanagan and Paul McCluskey for their help with the introduction; and Francine Weinberg for her help in editing all of the manuscript.

We thank Mary Ianora and Nancy Spitalnick for their typing, Joe Padial for helping with the production, and Deborah S. Aiges for her constant support. We are also grateful to our editor, Nancy Novogrod, and Jane West at Clarkson N. Potter for their support and advice.

We could not sufficiently thank Robert Bull for his contributions. Besides designing the book, he worked on it in every capacity. His efforts were enormous, and the book would not have been possible without him.

The excerpts from the writings of Flaubert and Du Camp are from *Flaubert in Egypt*, Francis Steegmuller, translator and editor. Atlantic-Little Brown, 1972.

Design, Layout, and Production by BULLWORKS . . . Inc.

Production supervision by Michael Fragnito.

© 1979 by Deborah Bull and Donald Lorimer.

Inquiries should be addressed to Crown Publishers, Inc., One Park Avenue, New York, N.Y. 10016

Printed in the United States of America

Published simultaneously in Canada by General Publishing Company Limited

First edition

Library of Congress Cataloging in Publication Data

Bull, Deborah.
  Up the Nile.

  Includes bibliographical references.
    1. Egypt—Description and travel—Views.
I. Lorimer, Donald, joint author. II. Title.
DT47.B8   779'.9'9162043   78-26418
ISBN 0-517-53512-2

Table of Contents

Foreword

The photographs in this book are wonderful. Many actually convey the sense of wonder the first photographers must have felt—seeing the Nile, the desert, the pyramids for the first time and describing them with the marvelous camera. And Egypt is probably best described with photographs. The strong light and solid monumental forms require a clear, precise medium. The daguerreotypists rushed there in 1839 just after the announcement in Paris of Daguerre's process. They were quickly followed by photographers working with paper and then glass plate negatives and eventually by tourists taking their own photographs with the Kodak.

The result was that at the close of the nineteenth century there were hundreds of thousands of photos of Egypt. Relatively few have survived, however. (It is ironic that the destruction of photographs through carelessness has tended to offset the advantages of their being multiple images.) The photographs reproduced on the following pages are among the best that have survived and together offer a splendid view of Egypt through the eyes of the finest artists who photographed there.

ANNE HORTON

Photographs, Sotheby Parke Bernet
New York

Introduction

When in the mid-nineteenth century photographers carted their cumbersome apparatus to Egypt, they were hardly entering uncharted territory. The land of the Nile had long been attracting travelers. More than two thousand years before, Herodotus had described the impressions from his trip in a book of his *History* devoted to the Egyptian monuments, customs, mythology, and religion. Plato, too, had written of Egypt, of the Athenian statesman Solon's visit and his discussions with the Egyptian priests. The region had been sketched and painted from life and from imagination many times. But the photograph, even in its earliest forms, made the journey up the Nile real.

Napoleon opened the way for the phalanx of archeologists, tourists, and photographers who would soon descend on Egypt when, in 1798, he took up arms against the Mamlukes, former slaves who had ruled Egypt in the name of the Ottoman Empire since the thirteenth century. He made certain to document the eastward expansion of his empire; he brought with him a team of *savants*—astronomers, chemists, artists, and engineers—headed by Dominique Vivant Denon, who methodically took the measure of the ancient land. Their findings were published in the massive *Description de l'Egypte* (1809-1813) and became the most complete documentation of Egypt to appear in the West.

Napoleon's presence was short-lived. By 1801 the British, fearing that their holdings in India might be threatened next, had ousted the French from Egypt. But Napoleon's initiative had been enormous: he opened Egypt to the West and tantalized Europeans with the *Description*, revealing wonders that succeeding generations of travelers were eager to see and evaluate for themselves.

And they came. Early adventurers like Giovanni Belzoni came to excavate and, in the name of archeology, conducted treasure hunts through the ruins. Exotic riches from the tombs of the pharaohs began to reach the European market. Fortunately, the plunder was often foiled by the very weight and mass of the treasure. But the findings of Denon's *savants* and of the early archeologists encouraged others, for whom romantic visions were being displaced by scientific curiosity.

By the 1830s the steamship had made Egypt more accessible, and the antiquities were being carried westward to Europe. Romantic painters, spurred on by the European passion for the East, traced the treasure back to its origins, making the trip themselves to draw the ruins. The visual documentation of the East was well underway in the lithography of William Henry Bartlett and others. But while he was in Cairo, the painter Willam James Müller remarked of his fellow artist: "He longs for some photogenic process to fix the scene before him."[1]

The need was answered in the 1830s with the development of the daguerreotype in France by J. Nicéphore Niepce and Louis J. M. Daguerre. At last it was possible to capture a detailed and accurate image by means of a mechanical apparatus. In 1839, just months after the process was made public, daguerreotypists arrived in Egypt. Among their number were Frédéric Goupil-Fesquet and the painter Horace Vernet; both had been sent by N. P. Lerebours, a wealthy Paris optician who was collecting daguerreotypes from all over the world.

Lerebours wanted to publish the views that Goupil-Fesquet and Vernet brought to him, but each daguerreotype was a unique image, and, as such, could not be reproduced. It was a direct positive

Frédéric Goupil-Fesquet. The Harem at Alexandria. The daguerreotype from which this engraving was made was taken on November 7, 1839, and is the oldest known photograph taken in Africa. The picture was taken in front of Mohammed Ali Pasha, who declared, "It's the work of the devil." The exposure for the picture was two minutes.

Frédéric Goupil-Fesquet. The Pyramid of Cheops. The daguerreotype was taken on November 20, 1839. This picture and the one of the Harem both appeared in *Excursions Daguerriennes* in 1840. Goupil-Fesquet had difficulty executing this picture, which took fifteen minutes to expose.

Hector Horeau. Abu Simbel. The daguerreotype on which this picture was based was taken in 1840 by Joly de Lotbinière. Horeau published this aquatint in *Panorama d'Egypte et de Nubie*, 1841.

image exposed on a light-sensitive copper plate. It was private. The viewer had to hold the daguerreotype at just the right angle to bring an image, which was beautifully reflective and filled with detail, into view. The plate was highly susceptible to scratches and light, and had to be kept in a velvet-lined case. So, in order to publish his collection of scenes from abroad, Lerebours hired engravers to copy the daguerreotypes. (Later, engravers worked directly on the daguerreotype plate.) In 1840 his *Excursions Daguerriennes*, a serial publication, marked the first time that views originally captured by a camera were published.

Other publications quickly followed. In 1841 Hector Horeau brought out *Panorama d'Egypte et de Nubie* which had aquatints made from daguerreotypes of Egypt taken by Joly de Lotbinière. The views published by Lerebours and Horeau, although one step away from direct photographic images, were immensely popular and excited interest in photography while adding to the growing fascination with Egypt.

By 1845 a new photographic process, the calotype, had been perfected and began to replace the daguerreotype. Developed by Henry Fox Talbot and refined by Gustav Le Gray and L. D. Blanquart-Evrard, the calotype was printed from a paper negative onto light-sensitized paper. By the early 1850s hundreds of prints could be made from a single negative, allowing, for the first time, the publication of original photographs. The paper negative was, of course, also lighter and less bulky than the copper daguerreotype plate.

Calotype prints could not provide the fine detail of daguerreotypes, but they were far superior in capturing a broad tonal range. They were more suited to the light-filled vistas along the Nile than daguerreotypes. In addition, the calotype process introduced a new flexibility, which allowed each photographer to experiment in his darkroom with different chemicals and techniques. Prints thus varied from photographer to photographer, giving a sense of individual style.

The publication of books illustrated with photographs was made possible by the calotype paper negative. In 1849–50 Maxime Du Camp received a commission from the French government to photograph in Egypt and, accompanied by his friend Gustave Flaubert, who had been commissioned to survey Egypt's economic potential, traveled to the Middle East. While Flaubert generally ignored his duty and passed his days in Egypt living "like a plant, filling myself with sun and light colors and fresh air , . . ." Du Camp took his commission seriously. He used his camera to document Egyptian monuments, taking frontal views, making accurate measurements to accompany his photographs, and usually posing a servant in his views to indicate scale. Du Camp was awarded the Legion of Honor, France's highest prize, when in 1852 these photographs were published in the book, *Egypte*, *Nubie*, *Palestine et Syrie*. It was the first important book of calotypes published in France.

Du Camp and Flaubert had made the trip up the Nile by cange, a boat that offered utility rather than luxury. The writings of these two men give some idea of what travel through Egypt was like in 1850. They described their boat, manned by twelve boatmen, who provided amusement with their songs and marvelous stories. Flaubert described the ceaseless hot wind, the khamsin: "We shut ourselves in; sand grits between our teeth and makes our faces unrecognizable." He gave impressions of color and light: "a glowing light that was like silver on the sea"; a sense of awe at the expanse as one traveled by camel; the silence; and the desert "looking scorched and iridescent."[2] There were bawdy accounts of meetings with the Arab women.

Other calotypists soon followed. Félix Teynard, a French civil engineer, went to Egypt in 1852 and again in 1869. An account of his 1852 visit, *Egypte et Nubie*, *sites et monuments les plus intéressants pour l'étude de l'art et de l'histoire*, was published in 1858 with some of the most beautiful calotypes ever taken. It was Teynard's only publication and extremely expensive even at the time. Although in many instances Teynard's subjects were similar to Du Camp's—both photographed the same monuments—their pictures differed vastly. It was Teynard's objective not to record architecture but to express its beauty. He focused his camera on complex shadows, intriguing corners, stunning but not necessarily relevant details. His pictures pushed the possibilities of the calotype to its limit, juxtaposing muted areas with brilliant washes of light.

Two other calotypists who traveled to Egypt in the early 1850s were J. B. Greene and E. Benecke. Greene was attracted to Egypt for its archeology, and his two-volume publication, *Le Nil, monuments et paysages*, appeared in 1854. Greene not only documented monuments and inscriptions, but he also recorded beautifully the Egyptian landscape. He died in 1856 at the age of twenty-four and never completed the work he intended to do in Egypt.

Little is known about E. Benecke, who seems to have been interested in photographing the people of Egypt. Benecke's achievement was exceptional. His pictures contrast dramatically with the portraits of well-scrubbed models, costumed and made handsome, taken in later decades to please the sensibilities of the European traveler. Only three or four of Benecke's prints survive. His pictures were published in small "keepsakes" by Blanquart-Evrard between 1852 and 1855.

Some of the calotypists who worked in the Middle East during the fifties were European travelers simply responding to what they saw. One such tourist was an English doctor named C. G. Wheelhouse, the doctor for a leisurely yachting party of titled Englishmen touring the area in 1849–50. Wheelhouse brought his calotypic equipment along and contended with trying to master the details of a new process as well as with explaining the camera to wary police. Wheelhouse's negatives were destroyed in a fire in 1879, and only a few albums remain. His handwritten notes survive and

J. B. Greene, c. 1853.
Calotype of the Colossus of Memnon.

offer a first-hand account of his use of the calotype process: "The photographs were taken by what was then called the Talbot-type process, a process only recently introduced by Mr. Fox Talbot and a first endeavor to obtain 'negative' pictures on *paper*, from which 'positive' ones could be printed at will, and as often as desired." In order to reduce the grain in his negatives, Wheelhouse explained that he saturated them with wax, a fairly standard practice. Although some of Wheelhouse's views were whimsical, others were surprisingly sophisticated.

A wealthy Irish landowner, John Shaw Smith, toured southern Europe and the Middle East from 1850 to 1852, and took 300 calotypes, some of Egypt. His negatives were not found until this century. Smith, like Wheelhouse, was interested in the calotype process as well as in documenting his tour, and he, too, took calotypes that were both personal records of his tour and achievements in a new and inexact field.

Louis de Clercq was a photographer with a strong archeological interest, and, in fact, accompanied a scientific expedition to the Middle East. His *Voyage en Orient* (1859–60) was five volumes of pictures, forty-one of which were of Egypt. (In his later years de Clercq was an avid collector of the antiquities he had photographed in the early 1860s.) It is interesting that de Clercq, traveling in the late 1850s and 1860s, continued to use the calotype process, which was no longer in widespread use. Perhaps he preferred the less-bulky paper negatives to the glass plate negatives that were generally in use by the 1860s.

During these early decades of photography, there were constant improvements both in negatives and in paper for printing. In 1850 Blanquart-Evrard, whose firm in Lille, France, printed large numbers of photographs, introduced albumen paper for printing. This paper, coated with egg whites and thus providing a smoother and more uniform surface, allowed for greater detail to show through in prints. De Clercq's calotypes, for example, which were printed on albumen rather than salted paper, achieved remarkable clarity.

The major technological advance of the 1850s was the introduction of the glass plate negative, coated at first with albumen, later with wet collodion. (These mediums were used to adhere the light-sensitive salts to the glass.) Wet collodion plates were virtually transparent, producing negatives that had no paper grain to soften detail. The clarity and detail of prints made from collodion glass negatives was electrifying; and the prints still retained the wide tonal range of calotypes. The new photographs were immediately popular, taking viewers away from their daily lives and transporting them to exotic places. Travel photographs grew in popularity, and the collodion process, which had been introduced by Frederick Scott Archer, was in widespread use by 1855.

The wet collodion glass negative was more permanent than the paper negative of the calotype. Hundreds of photographs might be printed from a paper negative, but thousands could be printed from collodion glass. Now the photograph could be mass-produced, and thus became cheaper and more accessible. Publishing of photographs, an enterprise that had begun with the calotype, grew into a large-scale business.

The first photographer of importance to use collodion glass plates in Egypt was Francis Frith, an English adventurer who had been a greengrocer, salesman, and printer before becoming a photographer. He made the first of his three trips to Egypt and the Holy Land in 1856. Frith realized the commercial potential of photographs of ruins and monuments; he knew that he could sell his work to an eager market at home.

There were drawbacks, of course. While collodion allowed for the production of large numbers of prints, the equipment was cumbersome, and the process difficult. The glass plates were not only bulky, but also fragile. Entire darkrooms had to be transported up the Nile and across the desert—cameras, tripods, boxes of heavy plates, jars of distilled water, chemicals, scales, funnels. Developing tents had to be set up within a minute's walk from the camera. First the negative had to be quickly and evenly coated with the sticky collodion. If flawlessly coated, then the plate was, in quick order, sensitized, carried to the camera, exposed, and taken back to the tent and developed before the collodion had dried.

In the desert heat of Egypt the collodion dried very quickly. Frith wrote of his difficulties working amid ether fumes in an airless tent in 130 degrees heat. He marveled at his own success: "Now in a smothering little tent, with my collodion fizzing—boiling up all over the glass the instant that it touched—and, again, pushing my way backwards, upon my hands and knees, into a damp, slimy rock-tomb to manipulate—it is truly marvelous that the results should be presentable at all."[3]

But Frith persevered, and his output was prolific. His albumen prints captured the clarity of the glass negative. His photographs

Vicomte de Banville, 1863–64.   Excavation at San. Banville was the photographer
accompanying an archeological expedition of the Louvre. The French photography
journal *La Lumière*, in its issue of May 30, 1865, said of this picture: "Clarity has
been forced to its limit." The photograph is an albumen print made from a collodion
glass negative.

depicted the images and moods of Egypt, its vast expanses of desert, and the monumental ancient ruins.

Frith returned to Egypt after his first trip, traveling, in 1857, to Palestine as well. Another photographer, Frank Good, is believed to have accompanied him and to have taken some of the landscape photographs signed in the negative by Frith, for these landscapes contrast markedly with Frith's stronger architectural views.

Then, back in England, Frith published two volumes of original photographs, each photograph accompanied by descriptive text, in an edition of two thousand. Frith's *Egypt and Palestine Photographed and Described* was the most ambitious publication of its kind to date, circulating a total of over 140,000 photographs, which were printed, fixed, and tipped into the pages by hand. To meet the demand for more pictures, Frith made the trip to Egypt once again in 1859, this time sailing up the Nile to the Second Cataract and continuing by camel beyond the Fifth Cataract.

The response to Frith's photos was overwhelming. The London *Times* wrote, "[They] carry us far beyond anything that is in the power of the most accomplished artist to transfer to his canvas."[4] The *British Journal of Photography* claimed that his volumes were "got up in a style that renders them fit ornament for any drawing room."[5] Frith also took views that were published as a series of mammoth prints, measuring as large as 49.7 cm × 38.8 cm.

Frith established in 1860 Frith & Co., a printing company located in Reigate, England. Over several decades the firm turned out an enormous quantity of photographs in a wide variety of formats—albums, boxes of pictures, stereoscopic views. These were suitable ornaments for any drawing room, indeed.

During the closing decades of the nineteenth century and continuing well into the twentieth, Frith & Co. was the largest photographic mass-production company in Europe. Photographers from the company were sent not only to the Middle East, but also over the British Isles and to the continent for images that were distributed in stationery stores and sold through catalogs. Frith's early views of the Middle East were those of one man; Frith & Co. offered images that were more romantic than Frith's earlier views.

The flow of Europeans into Egypt continued steadily, and photographers came with their massive equipment in tow. Among them were James Robertson, the superintendent and chief engraver at the Imperial Mint in Constantinople, and another photographer named Beato. These two men were on their way to photograph the Indian Revolt of 1857–58, and passed through Cairo and Giza, where they photographed with albumen glass negatives and made prints on salted paper.

Another photographer traveling in Egypt was Henri Cammas, who, with the writer André Lefèvre, published *La Vallée du Nil* in 1862. (Like de Clercq, Cammas used a paper negative.) When Cammas's photographs were shown in large format in 1863 at the fifth exposition of the Société Française de Photographie, they caused a sensation.

In the 1860s, when the Grand Tour of the Mediterranean and the Middle East had become fashionable, royalty also made the trip. In 1862 the Prince of Wales included the photographer Francis Bedford in his party to record his travels. Bedford's photographs were published that same year in four volumes, the full title of which reflects the itinerary of the tour: *Photographic Pictures in the Holy Land, Egypt, and Syria, Constantinople, the Mediterranean, Athens, etc., by Francis Bedford, During a Tour in the East, in Which, by Command He Accompanied His Royal Highness, the Prince of Wales*. The photographs, marked in the negative with the exact date on which they were taken, offer a marvelous historical record of a Grand Tour, typical of a trip taken by the royal and near-royal of the time. A contemporary observer remarked on the camera's role as a documenter of scenery and events: "The readiest and most effective pencil must have proved powerless to keep pace with the requirements of a journey performed under such circumstances . . . where every midday's rest, and evening halt, and dawning day presented a wealth of subjects to the skillful and artistic photographer."[6] Bedford's views were also available for purchase individually.

When the Prince of Wales arrived in Luxor, he was met at the dock by Lady Lucie Duff-Gordon. She, like others of her day, had come to Egypt for her health; caught by the spell of the East and having developed a special rapport with its people, she took up residence there in 1862. Lady Duff-Gordon, who remained prominent in the social scene on the Nile until her death from tuberculosis in 1869, was known for her lively letters home. When published, these letters did much to make Egypt an attractive place for an adventuresome Victorian lady to include in her tour.

One such traveler, Amelia Edwards, published an account of her journey in *A Thousand Miles up the Nile*, an evocative narrative of a trip in a dahabieh, a rather luxurious sailing vessel, up as far as the Second Cataract in 1873–74. According to Miss Edwards, Abu Simbel was swarming with tourists: a "fleet of dahabiehs"

Francis Bedford, March 16, 1862.   The Prince of Wales and his party at the Temple at Karnak. The Prince of Wales is in the center of the picture, the fifth person from the left.

studies in Constantinople; and Zangaki. Some of the most beautiful views came from the firm of Bonfils in Beirut. The signature *Bonfils* on a photograph may stand for Félix Bonfils, his son Adrien, or his wife Lydie; all took pictures for company stock.

Félix Bonfils had moved from France to Beirut in 1867 at the urging of his wife, who liked the Lebanese climate and had suggested photography as a livelihood for her husband. The venture proved successful. Within four years, Bonfils, reporting on his pictures of the Holy Land in a letter to the Société Française de Photographie, stated, "The collection I have put together consists of 15,000 prints and 9,000 stereoscopic views."[8] He wrote that he had a stock of 591 negatives. Bonfils *père* photographed until about 1877, when Bonfils *fils* took over the work. The number of pictures by Bonfils grew, and customers didn't necessarily know who had taken the view, just that it was by "Bonfils."

An enormous stock of photographs of the Middle East was developed to sell to the tourist market, and the monuments of Egypt were photographed from every angle, in every light. Company photographers often duplicated the views taken by earlier photographers, or, benefiting from improved emulsions that allowed for shorter exposure times, they devised new scenes complete with people and crowds. The companies, catering to the tastes of the tourists, offered posed costume studies of Orientals.

The photographs were promoted in the guidebooks of the day. Karl Baedeker's *Der Nil* of 1874 referred to the photographer Beato in Luxor, and other Baedeker guides from the 1880s and 1890s directed tourists to booksellers and shops such as Heyman & Co., next to Shepheard's, where views by Sébah and Lekegian were available. According to the Baedeker guide of 1898, "Good photographs are produced by A. Beato in Luxor; but even in Shepheard's and other hotels in Cairo, excellent photographs of Egyptian temples are sold at moderate prices. Those by Sébah are excellent." In this age of photographic companies, stocks of negatives often were switched from one firm to another. The new owner would scratch out the name of the original photographer or company and write in his own.

Then, at the end of the nineteenth century, the market began to fall off. Roll film now made it possible for tourists to take their own views with hand-held cameras that replaced the cumbersome equipment of the earlier photographers. No longer did travelers have to buy views by "professional" photographers. Calotypes had created the market, the collodion process had made it flourish, the dry gelatin process had made the demand for pictures simpler to supply, whereas further refinements in photography finally began to make the interest in commercial travel photographs shrink. Finally, the development of the half-tone printing process made the inclusion of original photographs in books obsolete.

The pictures of Egypt that have come down to us are very special documents of their time and place. Many more are still to be discovered. Invaluable pieces of archeological and photographic history, they are precious records of social history as well. The pictures enhanced Westerners' dreams of the East and fueled the fires of colonial expansion. The early photographers—tourists, archeologists, adventurers—captured an Egypt that no longer exists, but their photographs of that Egypt remain.

FOOTNOTES

1. Aaron Scharf, *Art and Photography*, p. 80.
2. From Flaubert's writing, translated and edited by Francis Steegmuller, *Flaubert in Egypt*.
3. Francis Frith, *Egypt and Palestine Photographed and Described*, Vol. I (Page "Early Morning at Wady Kardassy, Nubia").
4. Helmut and Alison Gernsheim, *History of Photography*, p. 286.
5. February 1860, p. 32. Cited in *The Real Thing. An Anthology of British Photographs 1840-1950*, p. 9. (catalogue)
6. W. M. Thompson, in the text accompanying Bedford's photographs, *The Holy Land, Egypt, etc.*, pp. 10-11.
7. Brian Fagan, *The Rape of the Nile*, p. 11.
8. Reported from the minutes of the meeting of the Société, September 1, 1871. Carney Gavin, "Bonfils and the Early Photography of the Near East," *Harvard Library Bulletin*, October 1978, p. 458.

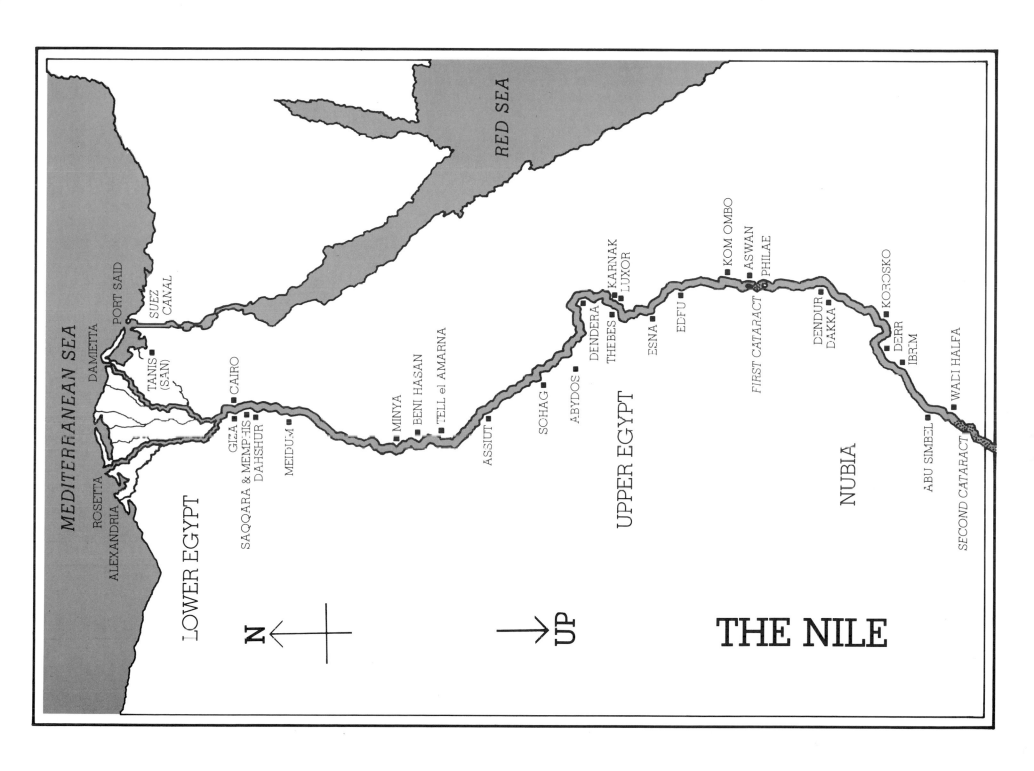

MEDITERRANEAN SEA

RED SEA

PORT SAID

SUEZ CANAL

DAMIETTA

ROSETTA

ALEXANDRIA

TANIS (SAN)

CAIRO

GIZA

SAQQARA & MEMPHIS

DAHSHUR

MEIDUM

MINYA

BENI HASAN

TELL el AMARNA

ASSIUT

SOHAG

ABYDOS

DENDERA

THEBES

KARNAK

LUXOR

ESNA

EDFU

KOM OMBO

ASWAN

PHILAE

FIRST CATARACT

DENDUR

DAKKA

KOROSKO

DERR

IBRM

WADI HALFA

ABU SIMBEL

SECOND CATARACT

LOWER EGYPT

UPPER EGYPT

NUBIA

N

UP

THE NILE

WHEN TRAVELERS arrived in Cairo, by way of the port city of Alexandria or Port Said, they found an Eastern city. The narrow streets were filled with bazaars, beggars, and mysterious veiled women, the very image of the Orient that the Western mind might have conjured up. The life and noise of Cairo were a far cry from the silence tourists would soon encounter on their journey up the Nile into Egypt.

Leaving the docks, tourists headed for lodgings in the newer European quarter of the city. As more and more Westerners poured into Cairo, an increasing number of places were established where they might stay in some comfort. The well-known Shepheard's Hotel near Ezbekiya Square was one, but there were others. Ensconced in these hotels, tourists made their arrangements, if they had not already done so, for hiring a dragoman (an interpreter, guide, and go-between) and for transportation to other parts of Egypt. Even in 1862 W. M. Thompson, an English writer, bemoaned the increasing Westernization of Cairo. Thompson was enchanted with the oriental city and disliked watching it become "more and more the resort of Europeans in the pursuit of commerce, of health, or of pleasure." But the mingling of East and West only added to Cairo's complexity and the intensity of its mood.

The old city, or Mouskee, was a maze of winding streets and alleys so narrow that sometimes the buildings on either side nearly touched. These structures, their windows covered with ornate latticework shutters, were in a state of deplorable disrepair. Dark alleys opened onto sun-filled squares; street musicians, soothsayers, water carriers, and cooks peddling unfamiliar foods shared the streets with donkeys, camels, and carriages. Cairo was dirty and exotic, unsettling and enticing. Its streets teemed with fascinating people who were vastly different in dress and physical type from any the visitor might have known before.

Nineteenth-century travelers in Cairo visited its mosques. They invariably went to the Mosque of Sultan Hassan, with its beautiful fountain, and the old Mosque of Ibn Touloun. Many of the mosques were not only houses of worship, but lodging places for the poor as well.

Cairo's crowning glory was the Mosque of Mohammed Ali, which was begun in 1824 on the site of a former palace and completed in 1857. It sat atop the Citadel and commanded a spectacular view. The old city had grown out from around the walls of the Citadel, which had been built by Saladin on the hills along the eastern side of the city in the twelfth century A.D.

Slightly south of the Citadel, the Tombs of the Mamlukes had been built along the slopes of Mount Mokattam. By the mid-nineteenth century these tombs, which had once been well kept, had also fallen into disrepair. The Mamlukes ruled Egypt from A.D. 1250 to 1805. Sent by Turkey to administer Egypt, they seized power and ruled until they were expelled from Cairo by Napoleon, who pushed them south. Finally Mohammed Ali Pasha, the "Father" of modern Egypt, killed them in 1811.

CAIRO

Frith Series, c. 1870.   View looking west across Cairo and the Nile to the pyramids at Giza.

2

P. Sébah, after 1868.   Worshipers at the Festival of Dosseh in Cairo. During this
religious festival dervishes lay prone as a sheik mounted on horseback rode across
them. Anyone injured was said to have been a sinner. After 1881 the sheik just
walked across the dervishes.

Frith Series, c. 1870.   Shepheard's Hotel. Situated near Cairo's Ezbekiya Square,
Shepheard's was especially popular with American tourists and British military
personnel en route to India.

Photographer unknown, n.d.   Interior of a hotel in Cairo.

C. G. Wheelhouse, c. 1850. View of a street in Cairo. The narrow streets afforded as much shade as possible from Cairo's brilliant sun.

6

W. Hammerschmidt, before 1860.   An Arab café with Egyptians relaxing and
enjoying coffee.

W. Hammerschmidt, before 1860. A copper shop, typical of the open-fronted shops in Cairo. Street scenes by Hammerschmidt, predating 1860, are unique in feeling. Because of the long exposure time that was necessary then, the camera was usually unable to capture subjects in motion; streets that were filled with people often look empty or contain only a few blurred forms. Hammerschmidt managed to have his subjects remain still long enough for him to photograph them without their appearing frozen.

W. Hammerschmidt, before 1860.   A spice shop in Cairo. Shops selling similar merchandise tended to be grouped together as bazaars. For example, there was a street of brass vendors, a street of spice sellers, a street of rug merchants, and so on.

W. Hammerschmidt, before 1860.   Camel caravans in Cairo.

E. Benecke, 1853. Nubian slaves
and slave dealer in Cairo.

Lekegian & Co., n. d.   Dervish.

E. Béchard, before 1875.   Arab woman. The photographer's name has been cut off, but other prints of this photo are signed E. Béchard or, in one instance, Bonfils. In the later part of the 1800s, one photographer often acquired the negatives of another.

12

Photographer unknown, before 1875.   "Howling" dervishes.

Zangaki, n. d.   Portrait of two Arab women.

These photographs, and the ones on pages 12 and 13, are typical of the studio portraits taken in the late nineteenth century. The subjects were directed to stand very still as they posed before the camera. The studies were popular mementos for tourists and were pasted in their travel albums.

Photographer unknown, c. 1870.   Group of donkey boys. Donkeys, a popular means of transportation within the city, were for hire in Cairo.

Photographer unknown, c. 1870.   Group of musicians, typical of those who performed on festive occasions. In addition to the tambourines, the *zummara*, a type of double flute, was popular.

Photographer unknown, c. 1870.   Portrait of a groom in elaborate costume. Grooms tended the stables and also ran alongside their masters' carriages.

Photographer unknown, n. d.   Rug merchant's shop. Shopping in Cairo involved bargaining, an expected procedure. The customer was seated, and then the wares were displayed.

Photographer unknown, n. d. Shepheard's Hotel with a group posed on the porch. The hotel's porch had been expanded and trees planted in front since the time of the earlier photo on page 4.

Maxime Du Camp, c. 1850.   A view of Cairo from the Hôtel du Nil, where Du Camp
and the writer Flaubert stayed in Cairo during their trip to Egypt in 1849–50.

Tancrède Dumas, after 1860.   View of the Citadel and the Tombs of the Mamlukes.

H. Béchard, before 1878.   Courtyard of an Arab house with the highly decorative latticework windows and crumbling walls that were typical of the architecture of Cairo.

H. Béchard, before 1878.   An Arab school
in Cairo. The schools, which were located
near fountains, were popular tourist attractions, and were featured in many contemporary guidebooks.

H. Béchard, before 1878.   A niche in the
Mosque of Sultan Hassan.

Photographer unknown, n. d.   Interior of the Mosque of Ibn Touloun. Built in A.D. 876-879, it is the second oldest mosque in Cairo.

397

Robertson & Beato, c. 1856.   Tombs of the Mamlukes below the Citadel. Robertson made a practice of including people—Westerners or Arabs for local color—in his pictures to give the viewer a sense of scale.

Attributed to Robertson & Beato, c. 1856.   The Citadel and the Mosque of
Mohammed Ali in Cairo.

P. Sébah, after 1868. An Arab cemetery, location unknown.

Robertson & Beato, c. 1856.   Arab tombs at the base of Mount Mokattam. The
Mokattam Hills are located to the east of Cairo.

TOURISTS VISITED the pyramids from Cairo. On a short stay travelers took an excursion to the nearby pyramids at Giza, with the obligatory ascent to the top of the Great Pyramid of Cheops and an inspection of the enigmatic Sphinx.

In ancient times the pyramids were covered by casings of limestone and red granite, which were dazzling when the rising sun set them ablaze. The ancient Egyptians could reach the pyramids by a stone causeway from the Nile. In the first half of the nineteenth century, tourists went from Cairo to Giza by donkey. After 1868 they were able to make the trip in a carriage on the road that had been constructed for the visit of the Prince of Wales.

All three pyramids at Giza were built during the Fourth Dynasty, within a period of about 100 years, between 2545 and 2457 B.C. The Pyramid of Cheops is the largest. The fact that this structure could accommodate Westminster Abbey, St. Peter's in Rome, and the cathedrals of Milan and Florence is an indication of its immense size.

At Giza tourists also saw the Pyramid of Chephren, slightly smaller than the Pyramid of Cheops, and a third pyramid, built by Mycerinus, of about half the size of the other two. These structures were built so solidly that a calculated attempt to disassemble them in order to use the stones for other buildings failed. In A.D. 1215 the Caliph Malik al Azis Othman started removing stones from the small Pyramid of Mycerinus, but he abandoned the project after eight months, leaving barely a trace of his efforts.

If tourists had enough time, they could explore more pyramids besides the ones at Giza. None was as grand as the three at Giza, but each was indeed worth seeing. Pyramids were built along the west bank of the Nile from Abu Roash, just north of Giza, to Meidum, about sixty miles to the south. Tourists covered the distance in day trips, traveling by boat from Cairo, then overland on camel or donkey.

About eight miles south of Giza, travelers came upon the ancient city of Memphis and the necropolis at Saqqara. At Saqqara tourists visited the Step Pyramid of King Neterkhet, or Zoser (2620-2600 B.C.), as he was commonly known. Zoser's Pyramid was built atop a square mastaba and was completed as a six-step pyramid. The monument, built by the architect Imhotep, went through several phases as a mastaba, then a four-step pyramid, and finally one of six steps. The overall height of the pyramid was approximately 200 feet. South of the Step Pyramid, Shepseskaf (2457-2450 B.C.), the son of Mycerinus, built the oddly shaped Mastabat Fara'un.

Tourists could also visit pyramids at Dahshur, about twenty miles south of Giza, where they would find two pyramids built by Sneferu (2570-2545 B.C.), the first king of the Fourth Dynasty. It is not known why Sneferu built more than one pyramid, but he worked on three in all—two at Dahshur and one farther south at Meidum. (The Pyramid of Meidum had been begun by a predecessor and completed by Sneferu. It was built as an eight-step pyramid over a core mastaba and then the sides filled in.) While his pyramid at Dahshur was being built, Sneferu adjusted the angle of its sides. The result was the oddly shaped, but aptly named, Bent Pyramid. The sides of Sneferu's other pyramid at Dahshur were built at the gentler angle used for the top of the Bent Pyramid. Long before the 1800s, most of this pyramid's outer casing had been removed, and because of the reddish hue of its inner core, it became known as the Red Pyramid. Also at Dahshur, tourists could find the remains of the mudbrick Pyramid of Amenemhat III (1842-1798 B.C.). Built during the Twelfth Dynasty, it was perhaps one of the last pyramids to have been constructed in Egypt.

Though some pyramids were built later, the Age of Pyramids lasted about 500 years from the Third through the Sixth Dynasty of the Old Kingdom. Forty-five centuries later, many of the pyramids were still standing for the nineteenth-century tourist to enjoy.

THE PYRAMIDS

Francis Frith, 1857. The pyramids of Mycerinus, Chephren, and Cheops at Giza. Because it is on slightly higher ground, the middle Pyramid of Chephren often appears to be the largest.

Maxime Du Camp, c. 1850. The Sphinx at Giza. Flaubert said of the Sphinx, "No drawing that I have seen conveys a proper idea of it—best is an excellent photograph that Max has taken."

31

Félix Teynard, c. 1852.   The north side of the Great Pyramid of Cheops. The first of the Seven Wonders of the Ancient World and the only one that has survived, the pyramid is 755 feet long on each side and 481 feet high.

32

H. Béchard, before 1878.   Ascending the Great Pyramid at Giza. A traveler paid his baksheesh (or tip, reported in Cook's guide of 1876 as three shillings) for the assistance of three able-bodied Arab men to push and pull him to the summit. The view from the top was well worth the money and effort: a vista of sand and pyramids, of the Nile, and of the city of Cairo.

From Mariette-Bey's gravures, 1878. Auguste Mariette excavating at Saqqara. Mariette, an influential archeologist active in Egypt from 1850 to 1880, is the bearded man seated at the left. Respected by the Egyptians, he was given the honorary title of "Bey." In 1878 Mariette published a series of gravures of sites that he had excavated in Upper Egypt. The photographer who took the pictures from which the gravures were made is unknown.

Photographer unknown, n.d. A view to the north from the top of the Northern Pyramid of Sneferu at Dahshur. The Mastabat Fara'un is visible in the background (left) and the Step Pyramid of Zoser is on the horizon toward the right.

From Mariette-Bey's gravures, 1878.   Mastabat Fara'un at Saqqara. This oddly shaped Fourth Dynasty structure was built by Shepseskaf. The building was never completed.

From Mariette-Bey's gravures, 1878.   Step Pyramid of Zoser at Saqqara. Built during the Third Dynasty by Zoser, this is the oldest extant pyramid and the first
important stone structure in Egypt.

Francis Frith, 1857.   A view of the pyramids at Dahshur from the east. The pyramid on the left was built of mudbrick and collapsed.

Francis Frith, 1858.   A view of the pyramids at Dahshur from the southwest, including two of the pyramids of Sneferu.

Frith 1858

From Mariette-Bey's gravures, 1878.   The Pyramid of Meidum. This pyramid was finished by Sneferu, and its casing stones collapsed leaving the inner core standing.

Photographer unknown, after 1881.   Excavations on the north face of the Pyramid of Meidum.

THE JOURNEY through Egypt was, above all, a journey up the Nile, a trip south on the river. (In Egypt the Nile flows from south to north, a fact that has confused travelers for centuries.) The time spent on the trip varied, depending on the means of transportation, but most itineraries included established stopovers. In the 1870s the journey from Cairo to the First Cataract, just below Aswan, took about twenty-one days by steamer. Under sail, the trip could take as little as six weeks or as long as twelve if the winds were unfavorable.

One hundred and sixty-seven miles south of Cairo the tourists came to their first stop, the Rock Tombs at Beni Hasan. These thirty-nine tombs, which were carved out of the rock for the nobles of the Twelfth Dynasty, were especially notable for being the only large mortuary complex as yet found on the eastern bank of the Nile. According to Thomas Cook's guidebook of 1876, the traveler was often met by "swarms of beggars and miserable donkeys—without saddles or bridles, the worst along the Nile." The beasts carried tourists on the half-hour trek from the river to the site of the tombs.

Another sixty miles south on the Nile, travelers came to the town of Assiut, the capital of Upper Egypt in the nineteenth century. Before the Egyptian slave trade was abolished in the 1850s, the principal slave market was in Assiut; after the abolition, Assiut continued to have a lively bazaar and market.

One hundred and twenty miles farther south, and a two-hour donkey ride from the banks of the Nile, tourists arrived at the ruins of Abydos, the traditional burial place of the God Osiris. At Abydos was the Temple of Sety I (1303-1290 B.C.), containing some of the finest carved reliefs from the period of the New Kingdom. This temple had an unusual number of chapels—not one, but seven, dedicated to deities. In fact, there was even a chapel devoted to the deified pharaoh Sety.

The next stop was Dendera, four hundred miles south of Cairo, two days' journey from Abydos by steamer, and three quarters of an hour's ride inland by donkey. Here, the late Ptolemaic and early Roman era temple was dedicated to the goddess Hathor and was used by the Greeks to worship Aphrodite. The Temple at Dendera had remained remarkably intact. Only the Temple at Edfu, farther south, was in better condition.

ON THE NILE

IN ORDER to undertake the voyage, it was necessary to secure transportation. There were three basic modes of travel up the Nile: the dahabieh, the smaller cange, and the steamer. If time was of the essence, then the steamer was the answer. It was generally twice as fast as the other boats and not at all dependent on the river currents or the wind. However, those travelers with the time and money sailed by dahabieh, the larger and more luxurious of the two sailing vessels. Lloyd's guidebook advised that "life on a Nile bark has a charm which seldom fails to operate even on the most inert mind. The traveler is perfect king in his boat."

If tourists were on their own, not traveling under the auspices of an organized tour, they first secured the services of a dragoman. If possible, they found the name of a reputable fellow from a friend; otherwise, they took their chances. The dragoman could make all the travel arrangements, as well as take charge of fitting up the boat. Not surprisingly, it was strongly suggested that a contract be drawn up between the travelers and the dragoman. A contract from 1856, published in Lloyd's guidebook in 1864, gives some idea of the kinds of arrangements that had to be made. The sample contract charges the dragoman with the responsibility for the provision of ". . . a spacious, comfortably fitted-up boat, with an awning and a small boat, and to furnish the aforesaid boat with beds and bed-linen, tables, chairs, china, glasses, filtering machines,

and all necessary comforts to first-class passengers . . . to provide all provisions . . . to give as many dishes for breakfast and dinner as the undersigned may demand . . . to engage and pay for the whole voyage a cook, a man servant, and an assistant to wash and clean the travelers' apartments."

The dragoman also provided for guides and donkeys at the sites visited. The sum to be paid was stated at the beginning, and the trip could be extended at the option of the traveler. (The sum for a party of four traveling from Cairo to the First Cataract over a period of about seventy days was about fifty-six pounds per person. Francis Frith's *Illustrated Queen's Bible*, published just a few years later, cost fifty guineas, or about fifty-three pounds.) Of course, the expense of the journey varied according to the size and relative luxury of the boat, the season of travel, and the extras that were furnished.

The boat had to be stocked with provisions which could be replenished at various market towns such as Assiut, Edfu, and Aswan. Contemporary travel guides give some picture of what travelers took with them. Books recommended the quantities of macaroni, onions, beans, nuts and fruits, coffee, tea, and wine that were needed to make the trip with some modicum of civility. When the wind was low and the boat was still, tourists could while away the hours in a drawing room atmosphere aboard their dahabieh and enjoy life on the Nile.

Frith Series, c. 1870.   Dahabiehs on the Nile.

Frank M. Good, c. 1870. Cabin of a dahabieh. The boat's cabin afforded the traveler refuge from the outside world. Meals were enjoyed in comfort at a well-appointed table. If the clock on the shelf is right, this photograph was taken at 1:05 one afternoon in Egypt, a century ago.

Félix Teynard, c. 1852. Rock Tomb Number 2 of Amen-em-het at Beni Hasan. Amen-em-het was the governor of the Antelope Province, or Nome, during the reign of Sesostris I, a Twelfth Dynasty pharaoh. There is a cane leaning against the column in the photograph.

Frith Series, c. 1870.   View of Assiut, looking east toward the Nile. Situated on a fertile plain, the town featured graceful minarets and palm groves. The road and bridges in the foreground crossed the Ibrahimiya Canal.

Louis de Clercq, c. 1859. Viceroy's Palace at Assiut, where Western travelers often docked their boats to pay a complimentary visit.

Zangaki, n.d.   Station Hotel at Assiut. The railway system began in the delta in
1855, and during the subsequent decades expanded south through the country.

Félix Teynard, c. 1852.   Tomb of Mourad-Bey at Sohag. The town was an
occasional stop for steamers taking on coal.

52

A. Beato, after 1862. Temple of Sety I at Abydos. The photos show the niches and wall reliefs between the chapels in the second hypostyle hall, a hall in which columns supported the roof.

Maxime Du Camp, 1850.   The posterior façade of the Temple of Hathor at Dendera, facing north.

Maxime Du Camp, 1850.   The birth house at Dendera, facing north.

Hadji Ismael was the Nubian sailor whom Du Camp placed by each of the monuments he photographed to create a standard scale of proportion. In order to keep Ismael perfectly still, Du Camp terrorized him into thinking the brass tube of the lens was a cannon that would kill him instantly if he was foolish enough to move. On returning one day from Dendera, Du Camp overheard the following conversation between Ismael and Rais Ibrahim, the captain of their boat:

"Well, Hadji Ismael, what news?" asked the rais as we boarded the cange.

"None," the sailor answered. "[Du Camp] ordered me to climb up on a column that bore the huge face of an idol; he wrapped his head in the black veil, he turned his yellow cannon toward me, then he cried: 'Do not move!' The cannon looked at me with its little shining eye, but I kept very still, and it did not kill me."

MAXIME DU CAMP, *Le Nil*

Félix Teynard, c. 1852.   The posterior façade at Dendera.

Louis de Clercq, c. 1859.   The Eastern Gate at Dendera.

FOUR HUNDRED and sixty miles south of Cairo, tourist boats docked on the eastern bank of the Nile at Luxor. Wide fertile land and gentle hills paralleled the bank on both sides of the river. Ancient temples intermingled with mudbrick houses and more modern stucco buildings. The gentle climate made Luxor a popular wintering spot even in ancient times.

The name *Luxor* derives from the Arabic El-Qusur, meaning "the castles." The site comprised one part of the ancient complex known as Thebes, which the ancient Egyptians simply called "the city." (The name *Thebes* came from the Greeks.) Luxor was a popular city for tourists, and contained a market that did a thriving trade in antiquities. By the late 1800s, it had become illegal to remove antiquities from Egypt, and Luxor was known for its forgeries. Chances were that objects being offered for sale there were fakes. (A method for antiquing scarab beetle amulets, for example, was to pass them through the digestive systems of domesticated geese.)

Ancient Thebes was comprised of three parts—what we now call Luxor and Karnak, on the east bank, and Thebes on the west. Thebes was the capital city and the home of the Eleventh Dynasty pharaohs after Mentuhotep II (2040 B.C.). Because of dynastic changes, the capital was soon reinstalled in the north, but Thebes later became a capital and remained so during at least a portion of the Eighteenth Dynasty.

A little less than two miles to the north of Luxor was the massive religious site known as Karnak, where tourists went in droves. The building at Karnak began in the Middle Kingdom and reached its peak during the New Kingdom, when soaring temples were constructed so high that it seemed possible to touch the god Amon, to whom the complex was dedicated, from their tops.

Across the Nile, on the west bank, was the city of the dead, now commonly known as Thebes. The ancients buried their dead on the west bank of the Nile, where the sun set, while the living stayed on the east bank, where the sun rose each morning. During ancient times the majority of people who lived on the west bank were those charged with tending the temples, involved in funerary rites, workers building temples and tombs, or those belonging to a garrison protecting the riches that were interred in the tombs.

The principal site that tourists visited at Luxor was the New Kingdom Temple of Amenhotep III (1403–1365 B.C.). Two groups of columns remained. Those at the south, which enclosed the second court of the temple, were said to resemble clusters of papyrus with closed buds for capitals. Those to the north were about fifty-two feet high with capitals shaped like open flowers. Tourists also saw an open court, enclosed on the north by a pylon, added by Ramesses II (1290–1224 B.C.). North of the pylon were two colossal statues of Ramesses, one of which is now in the British Museum, and until the late 1870s two obelisks; in 1877 one of the obelisks was removed and installed in the Place de la Concorde in Paris, where it stands today. Beyond, the avenue of ram-headed sphinxes led ancient Egyptians and nineteenth-century tourists alike to the Gate of Ptolemy III at the south of Karnak.

LUXOR AND KARNAK

J. B. Greene, 1853–54.   A view, facing northeast, of Luxor. To the left are contemporary dwellings; to the right of the palm tree is the Pylon of Ramesses II; at the extreme right are the minarets of the Mosque of Abn 'l-Haqqay, the Moslem saint of Luxor.

Vicomte de Banville, 1863–64.   A view, facing east, of the Temple at Luxor. The white building at the right is the house in which Lucie Duff-Gordon lived; a steamer and dahabiehs are docked at the shore.

A. Beato, after 1862.   The columns, from left to center, of the Temple of Amenhotep
III. On the right are stucco buildings built among and on top of the ruins.

H. Béchard, before 1878.   This gravure depicts the second court of the Temple of
Amenhotep III, commonly known as the Government Corn Stores.

A. Beato, after 1862.   Both this picture and the one opposite are of the colonnade of
the Temple at Luxor. The capitals of the column resemble open flowers.

Maxime Du Camp, 1850.

Félix Teynard, c. 1852.   The Northern Gate of Ptolemy III. In the background is the
Great Temple of Amon at Karnak.

John Shaw Smith, January 1852. The Southern Gate of Ptolemy III with the Temple of Khonsu behind. This gate is at the end of the Avenue of Sphinxes, which begins to the south at the Pylon of Ramesses II in Luxor.

Nº 93 Karnak Les Pylônes d'Horus.   H. Béchard

THEBES BECAME an important religious center under Mentuhotep II in the Eleventh Dynasty. The two gods of Thebes were Montu, for whom Mentuhotep II was named, and Amon. Amon was worshipped in a small sanctuary on the east bank of Thebes from the Middle Kingdom (c. 2000 B.C.) on. However, it was not until after 1554 B.C., when Ahmose I founded the Eighteenth Dynasty and the New Kingdom began, that the massive temple complex at Karnak in Thebes was greatly expanded.

The rulers of the Eighteenth Dynasty (1554–1305 B.C.) each added to the profusion of obelisks, pylons, and columns at Karnak. Intent on outdoing the work of their predecessors, they had Karnak rearranged and rebuilt by the standard practice of tearing down earlier buildings and replacing them. Queen Hatshepsut demolished the roof of the hall built by her father, Tuthmosis I, so that her two obelisks would show above the walls. After her death her successor, Tuthmosis III, had walls built back up to roof level in order to hide most of Hatshepsut's obelisks. His walls collapsed, but one of her obelisks still stands tall.

The Great Temple of Amon enclosed an area of about 54,000 square feet and remains the largest religious building ever constructed. Additions to the Great Temple began with a colonnade, enclosed by two pylons, with a court to the east, which was built by Tuthmosis III. The temple was expanded to the east and west by succeeding rulers. The building continued at Karnak until the time of Ptolemy XII, whose reign ended in 57 B.C.

Tourists who stayed in Luxor soon came to Karnak. Like all who have walked through it before or since, they were overwhelmed by its scale. In her letters from Egypt, Lucie Duff-Gordon conjured up a wonderful image of herself as a visitor wandering through the halls of Karnak in the moonlight.

The views here are of buildings in the central group at Karnak. The complex contained other clusters of temples and sacred lakes that are not represented in these pictures. People are hard to find in these photographs, but they give the viewer some sense of the staggering size of the ruins.

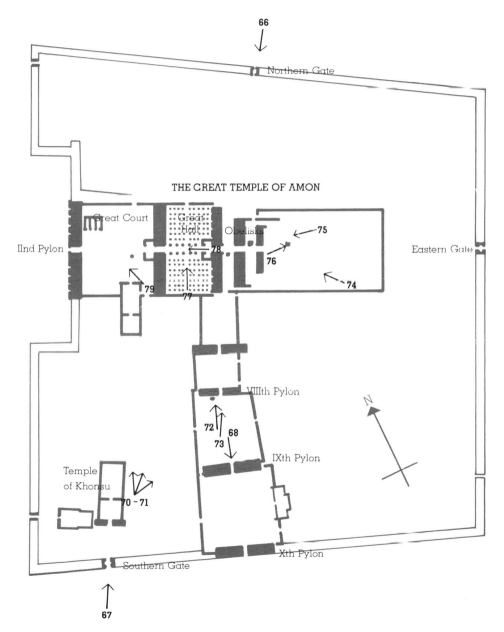

H. Béchard, before 1878.   Looking south through the ruined Ninth Pylon toward the Tenth Pylon of Horemheb.

This map shows the central group at Karnak. Page numbers are given, and the arrows indicate the approximate direction the camera was facing.

Vicomte de Banville, 1863–64.   A panorama of the Great Temple of Amon, taken from the Temple of Khonsu, part of which appears in the left foreground. The panorama is made from three separate negatives.

The first pylon is at the left; next is the solitary column still standing in the Great Court. The Great (hypostyle) Hall is in the center. Behind the Great Hall the top of the Northern Gate (page 66) is visible. To the right of the Great Hall are the Obelisk of Tuthmosis l and the larger one of Queen Hatshepsut. Farther right stands the Eighth Pylon of Hatshepsut. At the extreme right is the Eastern Gate.

Félix Teynard, c. 1852.   A close-up of the colossal seated statue of Amenhotep I
before the Eighth Pylon at Karnak.

Bonfils, after 1867.   The Eighth Pylon of Queen Hatshepsut, with her obelisk visible
behind.

N° 76 Karnak Vue prise du Nord-Est

H. Béchard

H. Béchard, before 1878.   The view, facing west, of the Great Temple of Amon at Karnak.

H. Béchard, before 1878. The Obelisk of Queen Hatshepsut. Made from pink Aswan granite, it stands ninety-seven feet high. The tip was covered in gold sheeting. This obelisk and another, which fell, were erected in the sixteenth year of Hatshepsut's reign. In the background stands the seventy-one-foot-high Obelisk of Tuthmosis I. A sliver of the Nile and the Theban Hills are visible through the Great Hall.

Note: The photo on the opposite page is from an original albumen print, which, as part of an extensive exposition in 1878, won a gold medal. Ten years later the collection of photographs was published as a large volume of gravures. In these gravures the images were all reversed. The view on this page and the one on page 78 are taken from that volume but are shown as in the original prints.

Félix Teynard, c. 1852.   A granite pillar, built by Tuthmosis III, with lotus motif from the Great Temple at Karnak.

John Shaw Smith, January 1852.   The fallen column in the Great Hall, facing north. The hall was immense, measuring 388 feet by 170 feet—large enough to enclose Notre Dame. The roof of the hall was supported by 134 columns. The columns in the foreground here are 42½ feet tall.

H. Béchard, before 1878.   A gravure of
the view (looking west) of the center nave
of the Great Hall. The roof here was thirty-
three feet higher than that of the side halls
and was supported by twelve sandstone
columns. The columns were sixty-nine feet
tall, topped by eleven-foot capitals. Six
men with arms outstretched were needed
to span each column.

A. Beato, after 1862.   Troops massed in the Great Court in the Colonnade of
Taharqo (690-664 B.C.). The pylon, which is 340 feet wide, may be the largest façade
of any religious structure.

THE TRIP across the Nile to the Theban necropolis on the west bank began at dawn. Tourists crossed from Luxor in small boats; once on shore, the travelers were carried by donkeys to the ruined mortuary temples and tombs that were in the hillside.

The first temple the tourists reached was Medinet Habu, built by Ramesses III (1193–1162 B.C.). Like other New Kingdom monuments at Thebes, the structure was immense and covered inside and out with hieroglyphics and stylized pictorial reliefs. These reliefs characteristically depicted Egyptian court life and celebrated the major events in the life of the person in whose honor the building had been constructed. The accompanying hieroglyphics narrated virtually everything that had happened during the life of the deceased.

To the north, tourists saw the seated Colossi of Amenhotep III, whose temple to Amon was across the river in Luxor. The two statues are over sixty feet high and mark the entrance to the king's mortuary temple that has since disappeared.

Farther on, tourists came to the Ramesseum of Ramesses II, or Ramesses the Great, who constructed enormous monuments up and down the Nile. The Ramesseum was almost as large as Saint Peter's in Rome, and included the Osiride Pillars, each a standing likeness of Ramesses, and the remains of a huge fallen statue of the ruler. It once sat fifty-eight feet high and was twenty-eight feet broad. A companion statue is now in the British Museum, where it was taken by Belzoni in 1817. Travelers could also inspect the excavations of the funerary Temple of Queen Hatshepsut at Deir el Bahari, which, begun by Auguste Mariette, continued into this century.

On July 5, 1881, in a deep shaft in the ground near the Temple of Hatshepsut, archeologists found a cache of forty mummies. They were the bodies of royalty, including Ahmose I, Tuthmosis III, Sety I, and Ramesses II. The mummies had been moved in ancient times to this communal grave to protect them from robbers who plundered the riches from the tombs in which royal personages had been buried. The forty mummies were removed from the shaft under the supervision of Emil Brugsch, a former assistant to Mariette, for the purpose of taking them to the museum in Cairo. Brugsch had the bodies loaded onto a steamer for passage up the Nile. As news of the find spread, Egyptians lined the river banks to watch the steamer pass. Men fired rifles in honor of their dead pharaohs; women, in keeping with ancient custom, threw clay and dust on their faces and bodies and rubbed sand on their breasts.

Tourists could complete their visit to Thebes by viewing the Theban Hills and the Valley of the Kings, where New Kingdom burials were in narrow shafts cut into the rock. A tour of Thebes as extensive as the one just described would have taken an energetic and dedicated tourist about two full days.

THEBES

Francis Bedford, March 18, 1862.   Long view of Medinet Habu, the mortuary Temple of Ramesses III. The view was taken during the Grand Tour of the Prince of Wales and his party. The Theban Hills are visible in the background.

A. Beato, after 1862.   A closer view of Medinet Habu.

Bonfils, before 1876.   The hypostyle hall at Medinet Habu.

A. Beato, after 1862.   The hypostyle hall at Medinet Habu. This is a slightly different
view from Bonfils's. The two photographers worked in Egypt at approximately the
same time. The Bonfils company was located in Beirut; A. Beato's studio was in
Luxor.

Bonfils, after 1867.   The wall at the right rear of the first court of Medinet Habu. The inscriptions are from the eighth year of the reign of Ramesses III. The line marked ▼ describes the bodies of the foe "slaughtered and made into heaps from head to tail."

A. Beato, after 1862.   This relief on the outside of the northern wall of the Temple of Medinet Habu commemorates a sea battle with the Sherden and Weshesh peoples.

Frith Series, c. 1870.   Looking north northeast toward the Colossi of Amenhotep III.

C. G. Wheelhouse, 1850.   An unusual view of the Colossi from the rear. Tradition
had it that the Colossus on the left in this picture sent forth a singing sound at dawn
and was sometimes called the vocal Memnon. Wheelhouse spent the night beside
the statue, and in the morning he proclaimed, "I heard it!"

Félix Teynard, c. 1852.   The left side of the base of one of the Colossi, decorated with reliefs depicting the unification of Upper and Lower Egypt, as signified by the twining of the lotus and papyrus plants.

Francis Frith, 1858.   A view of the Colossi. The middle finger of the statue on the left is four feet, five inches long.

J. B. Greene, 1853–54.   A view, facing southwest, of the Ramesseum, the mortuary Temple of Ramesses II.

Francis Frith, 1857.   The fallen statue of Ramesses II, known as Ozymandias to the Greeks.

My name is Ozymandias, king of kings:
Look on my works, ye Mighty, and despair!—PERCY BYSSHE SHELLEY

From Mariette-Bey's gravures, 1878.   The beginning of the excavation of Queen Hatshepsut's mortuary complex at Deir el Bahari.

Francis Frith, 1857.   A view of the Valley of the Kings. It was here that Howard
Carter found the tomb of Tut-ankh-amon in 1922.

THOUGH SOME nineteenth-century travelers were content to journey only as far as Luxor, many did continue south to the First Cataract. For this leg of the journey, they set out once again on the Nile.

The first stop was the town of Esna, thirty-five miles south of Luxor. Reputed to have been a pleasant, picturesque, and amusing town, Esna was where tourists could stock up on provisions, explore the bazaar, or, if they so desired, enjoy the pleasures of a colony of dancing girls, who were known to provide travelers with favors other than their dance. Esna, in addition to its other attractions, was reputedly the best place on the Nile to buy an Egyptian donkey.

Farther on, the scenery began to change. Wild game and pelicans became more abundant. The river banks here were steeper, the rocks were sandstone, and the strip of arable land was narrower. Thirty miles upstream from Esna the tour groups stopped at Edfu to see the large Ptolemaic period Temple of Horus. In the nineteenth century, the fine state of this temple, built between 237 and 57 B.C., was mostly the result of Mariette's efforts. The archeologist had evicted the people who were then living in it, removed the buildings that had been later additions to the site, and began to restore the temple's original grandeur. Prior to Mariette, it was said that a traveler could freely enter the temple but was accosted and threatened by the local population who demanded a large baksheesh when he tried to leave.

After a journey of about forty miles, tourists arrived at Kom Ombo, where the principal attraction was another Ptolemaic era temple. The temple, which had been added to during the Roman era, was dedicated to two gods: the Elder Horus, symbol of light, and the crocodile god, Sobek, symbol of darkness.

Another thirty miles up the river the travelers came upon the busy city of Aswan, at the foot of the First Cataract. It was an active commercial center, an important caravan stop, where goods brought from Africa were traded with goods carried by boat from Lower Egypt. According to Frith, there was a large traffic in wild and exotic animals, including "giraffes, gazelle-hounds, antelopes, various species of monkeys, apes and occasionally ostriches." Frith also noted that Aswan was a center for the slave trade, which in 1858 had recently been outlawed. (Frith observed that the trade had been "greatly reduced and conducted in a secret manner.")

Opposite Aswan, Elephantine Island drew tourists to see its Nilometer, which the ancient Egyptians had used to measure the height of the Nile floods. Visitors at Aswan could also stop at the nearby granite quarries, from which the ancient Egyptians had taken granite for the monuments of Egypt.

Above the First Cataract, which was about three miles south of Aswan, was the Island of Philae, reported to be a jewel. The island could be reached by going by donkey or camel from Aswan to the river above the cataract, and then by boat.

UP THE NILE

John Shaw Smith, December 18, 1851.   Pigeon houses in Esna. These structures were built of pottery jugs and mudbrick. The sticks that poke out from the upper stories were for the pigeons.

Bonfils, before 1876.   The Temple of Horus at Edfu. The most intact of any ancient
temple in the world, this building was constructed during the time of Ptolemy III (c.
237 B.C.) and Ptolemy IV and included additions until 57 B.C.

From Mariette-Bey's gravures, 1878. The Temple of Horus at Edfu, a view of the corridor between the temple and its outside wall.

C. G. Wheelhouse, 1850.   The Temple of Kom Ombo on the eastern bank of the Nile, dedicated to both Sobek, the crocodile god, and the Elder Horus. As seen here, much of the temple was covered by sand; its columns and capitals, in fact, stood 32½ feet above the ground.

Frith Series, c. 1870.   Dahabieh on the Nile, exact location unknown.

Francis Frith, 1858. Arab sportsman and cook, at unknown location. Frith photographed the evening's meal being presented to his cook, Vattel. The hunter had a European gun, no doubt secured from European travelers. Frith touted the virtues of his cook, proclaiming that "in the desert or on the Nile, with a little stove or two, some saucepans, and whatever he can get, [he] is unequaled."

Francis Frith, 1857.   View, looking north, of the landing place at Aswan. Frith observed, "A long line of native trading boats and of travelers' dahabiehs is moored along the bank which is sometimes almost covered with ivory and with bags of gum and other products from Nubia and Abyssinia."

Zangakı, n.d.   A view of the train station at Aswan.

A. Beato, after 1862.   The Cataract Hotel at Aswan, a stopping place for tourists in the late 1800s. The hotel, owned by the Thomas Cook Company, was situated opposite Elephantine Island and had lawn-tennis courts.

Maxime Du Camp, 1850.   The First Cataract, about three miles south of Aswan.
The cataract extended for about four and a half miles. An amusing pastime during
a visit to Aswan was to watch the Nubian children shooting the rapids on logs.

The most beautiful object my eyes ever saw is the Island of Philae. . . . I went and lay on the parapet of the temple. What a night! What a view. The stars gave as much light as the moon in Europe and all but the cataract was still as death and glowing hot.

—LADY LUCIE DUFF-GORDON,
Last Letters from Egypt

Henri Cammas, before 1861. The Island of Philae. The island was a religous complex dedicated to Isis, Hathor, and Horus. It reached its height in the first and second centuries A.D.—there is a relief of the "Pharaoh" Augustus paying homage to Hathor from that era—but as late as A.D. 600 pilgrims came to Philae to worship Isis.

Francis Frith, 1857. Dahabieh moored under the "Pharaoh's Bed" (the Kiosk of Trajan) at Philae.

Félix Teynard, c. 1852.   Reliefs from the first pylon of the Temple of Isis, the main
sanctuary on Philae. Among the cartouches of ancient Egyptian kings, there are
inscriptions in French, which commemorate the Battle of the Pyramids and the
expulsion of the Mamlukes.

Maxime Du Camp, 1850.   Relief of Thoth,
protector of Isis, in the temple on Philae.

THE JOURNEY into Nubia was not necessarily part of the standard nineteenth-century Nile tour. Tourists often ended their Nile journey at Aswan, and only the hardier travelers continued on into this more remote territory.

Although its borders have varied and were somewhat indistinct, Nubia was generally thought to begin at the First Cataract, continue past the Second (which is the approximate border of present-day Egypt and Sudan), and extend beyond the Sixth Cataract to Khartoum. Its connection with Egypt changed throughout the years, marked by coexistence, by Egyptian sovereignty and rule, and once by Nubia's control of Egypt.

South of the First Cataract the Nile was very different from downstream. Narrower and swifter, the river here ran past cliffs that at times soared as high as 800 feet, closing in on the edge of the water. The top of the cliffs was the Libyan Desert. In the stretches where the slopes of the cliffs were steep and high, the fertile land on the banks was sometimes as narrow as twenty-two to twenty-five yards. The dark granite cliffs added to the strongly contrasting effects of light and shadow in the Nubian landscape.

To reach Nubia, boats had to be passed through the rocks by pilots who were engaged at Aswan. The passengers went overland and rejoined their boat or changed to a different boat above the cataract. They then sailed past Philae, which they had probably already visited during their layover in Aswan. In 1875 the Thomas Cook Company initiated steamer service between the First and Second Cataracts. In their guidebook of 1876, they stressed the safety of the passage but suggested an additional "three days' margin in case of an unforeseen delay above the First Cataract."

About sixty miles south of Aswan, boats stopped at Dendur, on the west bank. The small temple, dating from the Roman era (30 B.C.–A.D. 324), was between the sandstone cliffs. The building was on the site of the tomb of two local princes who had drowned upstream, on the spot where at least one of the bodies was washed ashore. The placement of the tomb followed the ancient custom, reported by Herodotus, of burying anyone who had drowned where the body was found. The temple was dedicated to the Isis of Philae.

Some fifty-five miles farther south was the caravan stop at Korosko on the east bank. Travelers here took on needed provisions and possibly some of the many wares that were for sale as well. A tall peak topped by a Moslem saint's tomb afforded a view of the Nile Valley on one side and of the desert on the other.

The next stop was the town of Derr, famous for its delicious dates. It covered a fairly large area with mostly mudbrick huts, and included a ruined temple and some rock tombs. The last stop before reaching Abu Simbel was Qasr Ibrim, the final stronghold of the Mamlukes. A citadel crowned the heights above the Nile.

Western travelers found the Nubians exotic. They were dark skinned and described in contemporary accounts as extremely handsome and proud in their demeanor. The Nubians' dress was scant and, no doubt, tantalizing to the heavily garbed Western tourists.

The places that nineteenth-century tourists visited in Nubia no longer exist. After the dam at Aswan was built in the early twentieth century, Nubia was covered with water when the Nile was in flood. With the building of the High Dam and the creation of Lake Nasser in the 1960s, the area was permanently submerged. The government managed to save some of the centuries-old Nubian monuments, which they moved to higher ground or offered to foreign governments in return for assistance in the building of the dam.

NUBIA

114   H. Béchard, before 1878.   The Temple of Dendur.

P. Sébah, after 1868. Nubians in front of the Temple of Dendur.

These two photographs show the Temple of Dendur as it once stood in Nubia. Built during the Roman era under the reign of Augustus, 23–10 B.C., the temple was dedicated to Isis and commemorated the deaths of two Egyptian brothers during the fighting in 25 B.C.

To save it from the water that inundated Nubia when the High Dam at Aswan was constructed, the Temple of Dendur was dismantled and moved in 1963. It was floated down the Nile by barge and stored on Elephantine Island until shipped to the United States in 1968. The temple, including a pylon and terrace, which do not appear in the photographs, has been entirely reassembled in the Metropolitan Museum of Art in New York. It is the only intact Egyptian temple in the Western Hemisphere.

P. Sébah, after 1868.   A group of Nubians posed at the Temple at Dakka.

Photographer unknown, n.d. Portrait of a Nubian.

In his own country the Nubian seldom shaves or wears a cap except in one or two parts, but allows his hair to grow long and shaggy, soaking it well in castor oil; . . . a well-greased Nubian does not fail to rejoice in his shining shoulders. Nor are the means for keeping up the constant unction often wanting, as the castor-oil plant is much cultivated in Nubia . . . the women especially soaking their wonderfully plaited tresses in it constantly.
—*Murray Guidebook to Egypt*, 1880

J. B. Greene, 1853–54. Palm trees on the banks of the Nile. The exact location is unknown.

Félix Teynard, c. 1852. A caravan encampment on the Nile at Korosko. Scarcely a village, Korosko was a gathering place for caravans to the Sudan, and often there were as many as 2,000 camels there in preparation for the 200-mile journey to Khartoum.

Félix Teynard, c. 1852.   Derr, the "capital" of Lower Nubia. The rock tomb pictured
here was built by Ramesses II during the New Kingdom.

Félix Teynard, c. 1852.   A view of the citadel at Qasr Ibrim.

I N THE late nineteenth century, boats rounding a bend in the Nile confronted a staggering sight. Cut into the face of a sandstone cliff sat three seated figures of Ramesses the Great, facing the rising sun. A fourth statue lay shattered at the foot of an empty throne. These sixty-seven-foot-high figures were the most ambitious undertaking of Ramesses II, who was renowned for his colossal works.

The huge statues of Abu Simbel were carved into the face of the cliff, like enormous reliefs; a temple, extending back 180 feet, was carved inside the cliff. The entrance to the temple was between the huge figures. The temple was aligned so that a beam of light from the rising sun could reach into the sanctuary on only two days of the year, in mid-October and in mid-February. It was thought that the sunlight may have lit the sanctuary on about the twentieth of October in the year 1260 B.C., the thirtieth anniversary of the reign of Ramesses.

There was no mention of the temple in accounts before the beginning of the 1800s. In the earliest recorded exploration of the temple, Belzoni, probably the first to have set foot inside the temple since ancient times, dug away the sand to clear the entrance. He entered the sanctuary on August 1, 1817.

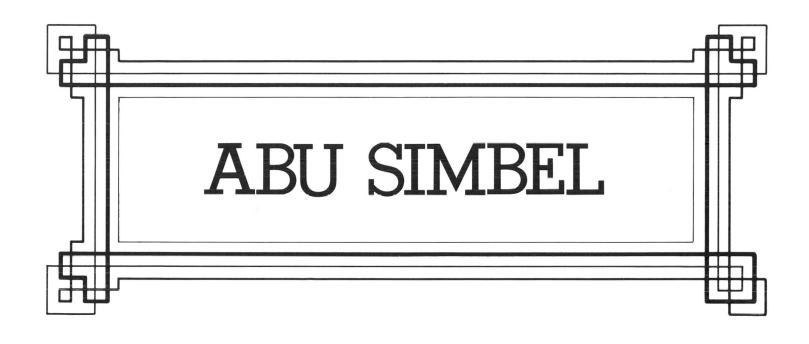

ABU SIMBEL

John Shaw Smith, December 1851.   Seated figure of Ramesses II.

Francis Frith, 1857.   The God Re-Horakhty over the temple entrance between the colossal figures.

Maxime Du Camp, 1850, both photos.   The colossal heads at the right of the temple. The white markings on the face at the right represent an early attempt at restoration.

A. Beato, after 1875.   Seated figures. By the time this picture was taken, enough
sand had been cleared away to reveal the missing head of the ruined colossus
lying at its base.

Félix Teynard, c. 1852.   A view, facing south, of Ramesses and of the Nile.

The Second Cataract, approximately 800 miles south of Cairo, marked the end of the Nile tour. A few intrepid travelers went on past it, but the trip beyond the Second Cataract left the realm of tourism for exploration. The rapids of the Second Cataract ran for about five miles; for the next hundred miles the bed of the Nile was sunken rocks.

Du Camp's view of the Second Cataract was probably taken from the top of Abu Sir, a tall cliff opposite the cataract that afforded an excellent view.

Maxime Du Camp, 1850.   The Second Cataract.

Abridged Chronology

The dates for Ancient Egypt are based on *Abriss der Geschichte des Alten Ägypten* by Jürgen von Bekerath (München-Vien: Verlag R. Oldenbourg, 1971). The spelling of Egyptian names is based on *Ancient Egypt as Represented in the Museum of Fine Arts, Boston* by William Stevenson Smith, Ph.D. (Boston: Beacon Press, 1961).

3000–2570 B.C.	**Archaic Period (Dynasties I–III)**
DYNASTY I (3000–2955)	Narmer Menes, first Egyptian king.
DYNASTY III (2635–2570)	Neterkhet (Zoser) (2620–2600) Step Pyramid at Saqqara.
2570–2155 B.C.	**Old Kingdom (Dynasties IV–VI). Capital at Memphis**
DYNASTY IV (2570–2450)	Sneferu (2570–2545) Pyramids at Dahshur.
	Cheops (Khufu) (2545–2520) Great Pyramid at Giza.
	Chephren (Khafra) (2510–2485) Pyramid at Giza.
	Mycerinus (Menkaura) (2485–2457) Pyramid at Giza.
	Shepseskaf (2457–2450) Mastabat Fara'un at Saqqara.
2155–2040 B.C.	**First Intermediate Period (Dynasties VII–XI)**
2040–1650 B.C.	**Middle Kingdom (Dynasties XI–XIII)**
2040	Mentuhotep II (2061–2010) Reunified country with capital at Thebes.
DYNASTY XII (1991–1785)	Sesostris I (1897–1878) Nobles interred at Beni Hasan.
	Amenemhat III (1842–1798) Mudbrick Pyramid at Dahshur.
1785–1554 B.C.	**Second Intermediate Period (Dynasties XIII–XVII)**
1554–1080 B.C.	**New Kingdom (Dynasties XVIII–XX), Capital at Thebes/Memphis/Tanis**
DYNASTY XVIII (1554–1305)	Ahmose I (1554–1529) Capital at Thebes; conquered Lower Egypt, expelled Hyksos.
	Tuthmosis I (1508–1493)
	Tuthmosis II (1493–1490)
	Hatshepsut (1490–1470)
	Tuthmosis III (1490[–70]–1436)
	Amenhotep III (1403–1365) Temple at Luxor, Colossi in Thebes, Karnak.
	Tut-ankh-amon (1347–1337)
	Horemheb (1332–1305)
DYNASTY XIX (1305–1196)	Ramesses I (1305–1303)
	Sety I (1303–1290) Moved capital to Tanis; Temple at Abydos.
	Ramesses II (1290–1224) Colossal works, Abu Simbel, additions at Luxor, temples in Karnak, Thebes, and Derr.
DYNASTY XX (1196–1080)	Ramesses III (1193–1162) Temple of Medinet Habu at Thebes.
1080–946 B.C.	**Third Intermediate Period (Dynasties XXI–XXIV)**
DYNASTY XXV (745–655)	Egypt conquered from the south by the Land of Kush (Nubia/Ethiopia) c. 730. Taharqo (690–664)
c. 670	Assyrians attacked.
DYNASTY XXVI (664–525)	Psamtik I (664–610) Unified country. Capital in the delta.
	Psamtik III (526–525) Last true Egyptian king, defeated by Persians in 525.
525 B.C.–A.D. 1805	**FOREIGN DOMINATION**
525–332 B.C.	**Persian Period**
DYNASTY XXVII (525–404)	Cambyses (525–522) Began Persian rule.
	Artaxerxes I (464–424)
c. 450	Herodotus visited Egypt.
332–30 B.C.	**Ptolemaic Period**
	Alexander the Great (332–323) conquered Darius III. On the death of Alexander, his empire was divided among his generals. Ptolemy became Ptolemy I (323–283).
c. 237	Ptolemy III (247–222) Northern and Southern Gates at Karnak. Began Temple of Horus at Edfu.
c. 207	Ptolemy IV (222–205) Finished Temple of Horus at Edfu.
	Ptolemy VI (180–145) Building at Philae begun.
	Ptolemy VIII (145–116) Temple at Kom Ombo begun.
c. 100 B.C.	Ptolemy X (108–88) Temple of Hathor started at Dendera.
	Cleopatra VII (51–30)
	Ptolemy XV (Cleopatra's son) put to death.
30 B.C.–A.D. 324	**Roman Rule. Roman emperors considered pharaohs.**
c. 25 B.C.	Augustus (27 B.C.–A.D.14) Temple of Dendur begun.
	Strabo, Roman historian, visited Egypt.
c. A.D. 130	Hadrian (A.D. 117–138) Visited Egypt.
A.D. 324–640	**Byzantine Era**
A.D. 638–1805	**Moslem Era**
c. 1200	Mamlukes seized power.

1249	Louis IX landed during the crusades and lost.
July 1, 1798	Napoleon (1769–1821) landed in Alexandria with 38,000 troops and 167 *savants* lead by Denon.
July 19, 1799	Rosetta Stone found.
August 19, 1799	Napoleon left Egypt.
1801	British expelled French. Established the Khedive (Pashas) of Egypt.
August 3, 1805	Mohammed Ali (1769–1849) became Pasha. Consuls set up by French and English.
1809–13	Denon published *Description de l'Egypte* in twenty-four volumes.
June 1815	Giovanni Belzoni (1778–1822) arrived in Egypt.
August 19, 1839	Louis Daguerre's (1787–1851) daguerreotype process delivered to the Academies of Science and Fine Arts in Paris.
November 1839	Frédéric Goupil-Fesque: Horace Vernet, and Joly de Lotbinière traveled to Egypt.
November 7, 1839	F. Goupil-Fesquet took the view of the harem of Mohammed Ali Pasha.
1840	N. P. Lerebours issued first of the *Excursions Daguerriennes*.
c. 1840	Henry Fox Talbot (1800–1887) introduced calotype.
1841	Hector Horeau published *Panorama d'Egypte et de Nubie*.
1843–46	Richard Lepsius (1810–1884) excavated and surveyed Egypt.
1846	David Roberts published forty-two lithographs of Egypt and Nubia.
1849–50	Maxime Du Camp traveled with Gustave Flaubert. Took calotypes in Egypt, Palestine, and Syria. (Du Camp's *Egypte Nubie* published 1852.)
1849–50	C. G. Wheelhouse, *Eastern Photography* an album of views.
1850	Albumen printing paper introduced by Blanquart-Evrard in Lille, France.
1850–81	Auguste Mariette (1821–1881) worked in Egypt.
1851	Frederick Scott Archer (1813–1857) introduced wet collodion process.
1851–52	John Shaw Smith in Egypt.
1852–53	Félix Teynard in Egypt. *Egypte et Nubie*—2 volumes, published 1853–58. E. Benecke in Egypt.
1854	J. B. Greene, *Le Nil, monuments et paysages*—2 volumes, published 1854.
1855	Railroad opened from Alexandria to Cairo.
c. 1856–57	Robertson & Beato. Views of Cairo and Giza.
1856–59	Francis Frith. Wet collodion. Made three expeditions to Egypt and Holy Land.
1859	Work begun on Suez Canal.
1859–60	Louis de Clercq accompanied a scientific expedition of Guillaume Rey as photographer.
c. 1860	W. Hammerschmidt in Egypt.
1860s	Frank M. Good worked for Frith.
c. 1860–80s	Tancrède Dumas worked in Beirut.
1861	Henri Camnras traveled with André Lefèvre.
1862	Antonio Beato arrived in Luxor.
March 3, 1862	Francis Bedford took his first photo in Cairo during trip with Prince of Wales.
1862–69	Lady Lucie Duff-Gordon (d. 1869) lived in Luxor.
1863–64	Vicomte de Banville traveled to Egypt with Vicomte Emmanuel Rougé to photograph antiquities for the Louvre.
1867	Lydie and Félix Bonfils moved to Beirut. Firm in business until 1895.
1868	J. Pascal Sébah opened studio in Constantinople.
1869	Suez Canal opened.
1870	Franco-Prussian War.
after 1872	Pre-sensitized albumen paper available.
c. 1875	Dry gelatin process introduced.
1875	England became major shareholder in Suez Canal.
1877	Adrien Bonfils became active in Bonfils firm. After Félix's death in 1885, Adrien ran company until 1895.
1878	H. Béchard won gold medal at L'Exposition Universele for views taken earlier in Egypt. Mariete (-Bey) published eighty-three gravures taken from negatives by an unknown photographer.
1880	Flinders Petrie (1853–1942) arrived in Egypt. Excavated in Egypt for forty-six years at most major sites.
1881	Gaston Maspero excavated Meidum pyramid.
1882–85	British fought dervish troops in the Sudan.
1885	General Gordon killed.
1889	Petrie opened Pyramid of Amenemhat II at Dahshur.
1889	By this year 12,000 Kodak roll film cameras had been sold. Photography was now available to everyone.

Bibliography

Abu-Lughod, Janet L. *Cairo, 1001 Years of the City Victorious*. Princeton: Princeton University Press, 1971.

Aldred, Cyril. "The Temple of Dendur." *The Metropolitan Museum of Art Bulletin*, Summer 1978.

Baedeker, Karl, ed. *Egypt. Handbook for Travellers*. Leipzig: Karl Baedeker (London: Dulau and Co.), various guides from 1874 to 1910.

Baedeker, Karl. *Egypt and the Sudan. Handbook for Travellers*. 8th rev. ed. Leipsig: Karl Baedeker (London: George Allen & Unwin, Ltd.; New York: Charles Scribner's), 1929.

Banville, Vicomte de, and Rougé, Vicomte de. *Album photographique de la mission remplie en Egypte, 1863–64*. Paris: L. Samson.

Béchard, H. *L'Egypte et la Nubie*. Paris: E. Béchard and A. Palmieri, 1888.

Borcoman, James. "Purism versus Pictorialism: The 135 Years' War." *Artscanada*, December 1974, pp. 69–81.

Bramsen, Henrik et al. *Early Photographs of Architecture and Views in Two Copenhagen Libraries*. Copenhagen: Thaning & Appel, 1957.

Budge, E. A. Wallis. *The Nile. Notes for Travellers in Egypt*. 2d ed. London: Thomas Cook & Sons, 1892.

Cammas, Henri, and Lefèvre, André. *La Vallée du Nil, impressions et photographies*. Paris: L. Hachette & Cie., 1862.

Ceram, C. W. *Gods, Graves, and Scholars*. Translated by E. B. Garside and Sophie Wilkins. 2d ed. New York: Alfred A. Knopf, Inc., Bantam Books, 1972.

Cook's Tourists' Handbook for Egypt, The Nile, and the Desert. London: Thomas Cook & Sons, 1876.

Cottrell, Leonard. *Egypt*. New York: Oxford University Press, 1966.

de Morgan, J., et al. *Haute Egypte* (2d volume of 1st series) *Catalogue des monuments et inscriptions de l'Egypte antique*. Vienna: Adolphe Holzhausen, 1895.

Denon, Dominique Vivant. *Description de l'Egypte*. 2d ed. Vol. III. Paris: C. L. F. Panckoucke, 1822.

Du Camp, Maxime. *Egypte, Nubie, Palestine et Syrie. Dessins photographiques recueillis pendant les années 1849, 1850 et 1851*. Paris: Gide and Baudry, 1852.

Duff-Gordon, Lady Lucie. *Last Letters from Egypt* (to which are added letters from the Cape) with a memoir by her daughter, Mrs. Ross. London: Macmillan, 1875.

——————. *Letters from Egypt*. Rev. ed. with memoir by her daughter Janet Ross and introduction by George Meredith. London: R. Brimley Johnson, 1902.

Fagan, Brian M. *The Rape of the Nile*. New York: Charles Scribner's, 1975.

Frith, Francis. *Egypt and Palestine Photographed and Described*. 2 vols. London: James S. Virtue, n.d.

——————. *Egypt, Sinai and Jerusalem. Twenty Photographic Views, with Descriptions by Mrs. Poole and Reginald Stuart Poole*. London: James S. Virtue, 1860.

Gavin, Carney E. S. "Bonfils and the Early Photography of the Near East." *Harvard Library Bulletin*, October 1978, pp. 442–70.

Gernsheim, Helmut, and Gernsheim, Alison. *The History of Photography 1685–1914*. New York: McGraw-Hill, 1969.

Horton, Anne. "Photo-Pilgrimages to Palestine." Unpublished paper, Columbia University, 1975.

Koning, Hans. *A New Yorker in Egypt*. New York: Harcourt Brace Jovanovich, 1976.

Lloyd's Handbook for Travellers in Egypt. (Literary-artistic section of the Austrian Lloyd.) Translated by W. C. Wrankmore. 2d ed. Trieste, 1864.

Mariette-Bey, Auguste. *Voyage dans la Haute-Egypte*. 2d ed. Paris: H. Welter, 1893.

Moorehead, Alan. *The Blue Nile*. New York: Harper & Row, 1962.

Murray, John. *A Handbook for Travellers in Lower and Upper Egypt*. 6th ed. London: John Murray, 1880.

Newhall, Beaumont. *The History of Photography*. New York: The Museum of Modern Art, 1964.

Pollack, Peter. *The Picture History of Photography*. New York: Harry N. Abrams, 1977.

Porter, Bertha, and Moss, Rosalind. *Topographical Bibliography of Ancient Egyptian Hieroglyphic Texts, Reliefs, and Paintings*. 2d ed., revised and augmented by Jaromir Málek. London: Oxford University Press, 1974.

Scharf, Aaron. *Art and Photography*. Harmondsworth: Penguin Press, 1968.

Sébah, J. P. *Catalogue général de la collection des vues de la Haute et Basse-Egypte et de la Nubie*, n.d.

Steegmuller, Francis, translator and editor. *Flaubert in Egypt*. Boston: Atlantic–Little, Brown, 1972.

Teynard, Félix. *Egypte et Nubie, sites et monuments les plus intéressants pour l'étude de l'art et de l'histoire*. 2 vols. Paris: Goupil et Cie., 1858.

Thompson, W. M. Text and introduction to *The Holy Land, Egypt, etc. Forty-eight photographs by Francis Bedford*. London: Day & Son and The German Gallery, 1862.

University of Chicago, Oriental Institute. *Medinet Habu*. Vol I. The Epigraphic Survey, Harold Haydon Nelson, Field Director. Chicago: University of Chicago Press, 1930.

University of Chicago, Oriental Institute and the Egypt Exploration Society. *The Temple of King Sethos I at Abydos*. Vol IV. Sir Alan Gardner, ed. Chicago: University of Chicago Press, 1958.

Welling, William. *Collectors' Guide to Nineteenth Century Photographs*. New York: Macmillan, 1976.

Exhibition Catalogues

Arts Council of Great Britain. *The Real Thing. An Anthology of British Photographs 1840–1950*. 1975.

Arts Council of Great Brittian. *From Today Painting Is Dead. The Beginnings of Photography*. Victoria and Albert Museum, 1972.

Jammes, André, catalogue and essay. *French Primitive Photography*. Introduction by Minor White; commentary by Robert Sobieszek. New York: Aperture, 1970.

Jammes, André, and Jammes, Marie-Thérèse. *The First Century of Photography, Niepce to Atget, from the collection of André Jammes*. Introduction by David Travis. Chicago: The Art Institute of Chicago, 1977.

Jammes, André, and Jammes, Marie-Thérèse. *En Egypte au temps de Flaubert: 1839–1860, les premiers photographes*. Kodak-Pathé. Paris, 1976.

Naef, Weston. *Early Photographers in Egypt and the Holy Land 1849–1870*. New York: The Metropolitan Museum of Art, September, 1973.

University of New Mexico, Art Museum. *Nineteenth Century Photographs from the Collection*. Preface by Beaumont Newhall and Introduction by Van Deren Coke.

Index of Plates and Sources

All sizes are given in centimeters, width preceding height. All prints, unless otherwise noted, are albumen prints. The descriptions and spellings, where available, were taken from descriptions accompanying the photographs, either written on the mounts, in the negatives, or in accompanying text. These descriptions are in quotation marks and the spellings may vary from those elsewhere in the text.

TIAN AND CLASSICAL ART, The Brooklyn Museum.

p. *26*, "32B: Cimétiers Arabes" (27 × 21) Courtesy KIMMEL-COHN, New York.

p. *115*, "No. 119: Nubiens de Dandour" (22 × 26) Private collection.

p. *116*, "29: Groupe de Nubiens à Dakièh" (27 × 21) Courtesy DEPARTMENT OF EGYPTIAN AND CLASSICAL ART, The Brooklyn Museum.

Smith, John Shaw (1811–73)

All pictures 22.9 × 18 (salted paper prints) GERNSHEIM COLLECTION. HUMANITIES RESEARCH CENTER, The University of Texas at Austin.

p. *67*, "Great Gate at Karnac."

p. *77*, "Interior of Great Hall, Karnac."

p. *98*, "Pigeon Houses of Pottery and Houses, Esne, Egypt."

p. *125*, "Great Temple at Aboo Simbel."

p. *126*, "Great Temple at Aboo Simbel."

Teynard, Félix (1817–92)

From *Egypte et Nubia, Vols. I and II* (salted paper prints).

p. *32*, Pl. 9: "Djizeh—Pyramide de Chéops" (31 × 24.7) BIBLIOTHÈQUE NATIONALE, Paris.

p. *47*, Pl. 13: "Béni Haçan" (30.8 × 24.6) THE BRITISH LIBRARY.

p. *51*, Pl. 21: "Souàdj" (30.8 × 24) BIBLIOTHÈQUE NATIONALE, Paris.

p. *56*, Pl. 24: "Dendérah" (30.8 × 24) BIBLIOTHÈQUE NATIONALE, Paris.

p. *66*, Pl. 64: "Karnak (Thèbes)" (30.5 × 23.8) BIBLIOTHÈQUE NATIONALE, Paris.

p. *72*, Pl. 65: "Karnak (Thèbes)" (30.8 × 24.4) BIBLIOTHÈQUE NATIONALE, Paris.

p. *76*, Pl. 60: "Karnak (Thèbes)" (13.8 × 27) BIBLIOTHEQUE NATIONALE, Paris.

p. *90*, Pl. 41: "Gournah (Thèbes) Colosse de Gauche" (30.5 × 24.3) BIBLIOTHÈQUE NATIONALE, Paris.

p. *110*, Pl. 98: "Ile de Fìleh" (30.8 × 24) BIBLIOTHÈQUE NATIONALE, Paris.

p. *119*, Pl. 133: "Korosko" (29.5 × 23.8) Courtesy PETER COFFEEN.

p. *120*, Pl. 140: "Deir" (30.5 × 23.9) BIBLIOTHÈQUE NATIONALE, Paris.

p. *121*, Pl. 142: "Ibrim" (30.5 × 24) THE BRITISH LIBRARY.

p. *129*, Pl. 153: "Abou-Sembil" (30.5 × 23.8) BIBLIOTHÈQUE NATIONALE, Paris.

Wheelhouse, C. G. (n.d.)

From an album, "Eastern Photography" (salted paper prints), all reproduced actual size. From THE ROYAL PHOTOGRAPHIC SOCIETY Collection.

p. *6*, 38: "Street view, Cairo" (10.8 × 14.5).

p. *89*, 56: "Vocal Memnon from Behind" (20.5 × 15.6).

p. *101*, 58: "Kom Ombos" (20.8 × 15.4).

Zangaki (n.d.)

p. *13*, 750: Two Women (21.5 × 23.7) Courtesy MARCUSE PFEIFER Gallery, New York.

p. *50*, "No. 646 Assiout" (28 × 21.5) Courtesy DEPARTMENT OF EGYPTIAN AND CLASSICAL ART, The Brooklyn Museum.

p. *105*, "No. 754 Assouan Gare du chemin de fer" (28.1 × 21.2) Courtesy DEPARTMENT OF EGYPTIAN AND CLASSICAL ART, The Brooklyn Museum.

Photographer unknown

p. *5*, Hotel Interior (26 × 19.8) Courtesy of PETER COFFEEN.

p. *13*, "Howling" Dervishes (18.8 x 25.1) Private collection.

p. *14*, Donkey Boys (24.6 × 18.7) Private collection.

p. *15*, Musicians (18.5 × 24.9) Private collection.

p. *15*, Groom (16 × 20.8) Private collection.

p. *16*, Rug Merchants (26.8 × 19.6) Courtesy DEPARTMENT OF EGYPTIAN AND CLASSICAL ART, The Brooklyn Museum.

p. *17*, Shepheard's Hotel (26 × 20) Courtesy DEPARTMENT OF EGYPTIAN AND CLASSICAL ART, The Brooklyn Museum.

p. *23*, 397: Mosquee Touloun (27 × 21) Courtesy KIMMEL-COHN, New York.

p. *35*, North from Dashur (34.5 × 26.5) Courtesy DEPARTMENT OF EGYPTIAN AND CLASSICAL ART, The Brooklyn Museum.

p. *41*, Digging at Meidum (34 × 26.5) Courtesy DEPARTMENT OF EGYPTIAN AND CLASSICAL ART, The Brooklyn Museum.

p. *117*, Type of Nubian (17.9 × 22.2) Courtesy DEPARTMENT OF EGYPTIAN AND CLASSICAL ART, The Brooklyn Museum.

Index of Sites

Francis Frith, 1857.   Crocodile on a sand-bank.

The text was set in Memphis Light by A & S Graphics, Inc., Wantagh, New York. The photographs were printed in duotone by Halliday Lithograph Corporation, West Hanover, Massachusetts, on Warren's Lustro Offset Enamel Dull supplied by Lindenmeyr Paper Corporation. The book was bound by A. Horowitz & Son, Fairfield, New Jersey. *Up the Nile* was designed by Robert Bull.